INTRODUCTION

THE NOVEL CORONAVIRUS created both a humanitarian and an economic crisis. When it ends, we will mourn the lives lost, but we need not long mourn the economic costs. The economy will rebound, and with astounding speed, if capitalism is allowed to work its magic.

First and foremost, we need to help people and businesses through this crisis. But when the crisis is over the economy must reignite, and for that we need policies that encourage businesses to grow and hire, rather than policies that encourage government dependence and discourage work.

That's the lesson of President Obama's tenure in office compared to President Trump's. The Obama administration discouraged growth by raising taxes and expanding the government through laws and regulations to an extent FDR would have envied. Businesses were reluctant to grow and create jobs.

[

As a result, Obama presided over eight years of anemic growth and a stagnant labor market.

President Trump passed a tax cut for people and businesses and took a machete to the jungle of rules and regulations promulgated under Obama. The economy grew and the labor market flourished. In fact, before COVID-19 hit the United States, we had the strongest labor market in modern history.

That labor market strength was due to President Trump's business-friendly economic policies that allowed capitalism to work its genius. Perhaps as important was the signal his policies sent: The Obama era of government burden was at an end. Businesses could invest in a predictable environment, without fear that their own government would attack their success.

The same recipe that produced the strongest labor market in modern history can restore the wealth we lost because of the pandemic. If government helps people now, as it should, but otherwise gets out of the way

> *President Trump passed a tax cut for people and businesses and took a machete to the jungle of rules and regulations promulgated under Obama.*

and empowers the private sector, the impact of the virus will be a short-term hit from which we will recover rapidly. If the government keeps its heavy hand on the economy, we may never fully recover.

The most compassionate thing we can do for all Americans is restart the economy – once we are no longer at risk. We need our stores, restaurants, and hotels open, our manufacturers manufacturing, and our consumers once again consuming. That requires incentivizing investors to invest, businesses to hire, and workers to work. Otherwise, we will end up with years of Obama-style stagnation –

what he called the "new normal" – rather than the growth in jobs, wages, and prosperity that became the norm under President Trump.

Unfortunately, the Coronavirus crisis put the brakes on that growth and required increased government action to address its impact. As in any crisis, many individuals and families are suffering disproportionately and through no fault of their own. As a nation, we are committed to guarding people against disaster, and we should assist them generously. The government has moved on a bipartisan basis quickly to help these people.

American businesses are also suffering and in need of assistance.

For some, the government's financial assistance of various businesses harkens back to the bailouts following the Great Recession. But it is important to keep in mind that, unlike the Great Depression, the Savings and Loan crisis of the late 1980s, the Tech Bubble of 2000, or the 2007 real estate bubble that led to the Great Recession, the current economic crisis was not due to speculation or excessive risk taking by businesses, investors, or our financial institutions. It was due to a government-driven economic shutdown in response to a global pandemic.

America's business community is in serious trouble through no fault of its own. The assistance it receives is in no way a "bailout." Rather, it is compensation for the government taking away its ability to operate. Very few businesses have sufficient cash on hand to withstand a months-long period of virtually no revenue, yet that is what the government is forcing businesses to do.

As a result, the government has properly moved in the direction of protecting both our businesses and the jobs they create with massive but short-term programs designed to address the lack of capital and financial liquidity during the crisis.

Treating the fight against the Coronavirus as an effort akin to war, both President Trump and Congress have effectively employed the tools available to government. Unfortunately, some Progressives are already arguing that our response to the Coronavirus proves the need for big government. As if the need for massive state intervention to address the pandemic justifies the Left's entire collectivist belief system.

It doesn't.

Government is essential in any functioning capitalist economy to, among other things, protect property and contract rights, keep the peace, organize major infrastructure projects, provide for national defense, help those who cannot support themselves, and assist people and commerce in a disaster. A pandemic certainly qualifies as a disaster. However, to use one problem government should address as the basis for arguing that government is well suited to address every problem is sophistry, pure and simple.

Nonetheless, statists attempt to expand government in nearly every crisis – not wishing to "let a serious crisis go to waste" as Obama's chief of staff Rahm Emanuel once famously stated. House Majority Whip James

Clyburn (D-SC) echoed Emanuel's statement by describing the Coronavirus crisis as "a tremendous opportunity to restructure things to fit our vision." That vision is a post-pandemic socialist future in which the government, rather than the private sector, controls our economy.

But when it comes to growing the economy, big government policies have consistently proven inferior to policies that empower free markets. Just compare the prosperous capitalist economies in Singapore, Hong Kong, Taiwan, and South Korea with the destitute socialist economies in North Korea, Cuba, and Venezuela. The reality is that, in every corner of the world, free market economies have delivered far greater prosperity than government-run economies.

Contrary to what Progressives will tell you, Scandinavian nations like Denmark and Sweden are not exceptions to this rule. These nations have large safety nets, but they also have vital free markets. In fact the Heritage

Foundation's 2020 Index of Economic Freedom ranks Denmark the eighth and Sweden the twenty-second freest economies in the world – out of the 180 it ranks. The United States ranks seventeenth.

You can argue about the costs of their expansive welfare systems and the point at which tax rates become so high as to penalize work, reduce individual initiative, and drive away investors. In fact, both Denmark and Sweden have been debating exactly those issues for years – and reducing taxes and social welfare programs as a result.

It is doubtful Americans would stomach the high income taxes on almost everyone (not just the wealthy) and regressive value-

---

Before COVID-19 hit the United States, we had the strongest labor market in modern history.

---

added taxes in excess of 20 percent that are required to pay for Scandinavian-style welfare systems. But you know Denmark and Sweden must have capitalist free market economies because only free market economies can even come close to producing the wealth necessary to sustain such expansive welfare programs.

So, what should happen in the United States when this crisis ends? How do we get the economy roaring again?

The right prescription going forward is the one that worked so well over the last three years, and indeed for the last two hundred years, in the most dynamic free market the world has ever seen. When this crisis ends, all we need to do to restart our economy is return to what produced the Trump boom in the first place – regulatory relief, certainty, and tax policies that allow individuals and businesses to keep most of what they earn.

The economy will rebound with astounding speed if – and only if – we put our faith in the vast potential of enterprising individuals in a free market economy. That will require ending much of what the government is doing to address the Coronavirus crisis and resisting the inevitable urge for government to keep doing more after the crisis abates. Rather than restructuring "things to fit" a misguided progressive "vision," as Congressman Clyburn would prefer, it will require acknowledging that a government which grows to address a crisis must recede when that crisis ends.

In other words, bigger government isn't the path to economic renewal. It is the obstacle.

Unfortunately, restoring these pre-pandemic policies may be more difficult than it sounds. As President Reagan once said: "No government ever voluntarily reduces itself in size." But that's exactly what must happen if we are to restart our economy and return our nation to the widespread and unprecedented prosperity we experienced before COVID-19 reached American shores.

Obama's "New Normal" vs. The Trump Norm

To understand the magnitude of the negative impact President Obama's policies had on the economy, and the labor market in particular, it's important to understand what his administration believed would happen when he assumed office – and just how wrong it was.

Milton Friedman recognized in the early 1960s that the deeper the recession, the stronger – and faster – the recovery should be. In early 2009, the country was nearing the end of a deep recession and, because of that economic cycle, President Obama's economic team expected a strong and rapid recovery – almost regardless of what they did.

In 2010, the Obama White House forecast GDP growth would "accelerate in 2011 to 3.8 percent" and "exceed 4 percent per year in 2012–2014." Given the depth of the Great Recession, the White House forecast seemed conservative. In the other ten post–World War II recoveries, GDP grew at an average of

4.3 percent. But, for Obama, it never happened.

In fact, under President Obama, GDP failed to achieve a single calendar year of 3 percent growth. For the seven post-recession years of his presidency, GDP growth averaged 2.2 percent. His final year in office, GDP grew at a near-recessionary 1.6 percent.

The labor market – and American workers – suffered.

When Obama took office, the unemployment rate was 7.8 percent. Almost immediately, his economic advisors issued a report arguing for massive government stimulus to revitalize the economy, claiming that with this "stimulus" spending unemployment would remain below 8 percent. Obama described the report as a "rigorous analysis so that the American people can see exactly what this plan will mean for their families, their communities, and our economy."

The report was arguably even more inaccurate than his administration's GDP forecast.

In February, without a single Republican

vote in the House and a meager three Republican votes in the Senate, the Democrats passed a Keynesian style "stimulus" bill authorizing over $800 billion in federal spending for supposedly "shovel-ready" projects.

It stimulated nothing.

Obama would chuckle two years later when admitting that "'Shovel-ready' was not as – uh – shovel-ready as we expected." Failed investments in government-selected "winners" like Fisker and Solyndra were clear evidence of the so-called "stimulus" bill's utter failure.

As for the unemployment rate, it spiked to 10 percent within months. It would be forty-three months before it dropped below the promised 8 percent.

When the unemployment rate did decline, it wasn't due to any Keynesian stimulus. Rather, it was due to people dropping out of the labor force – either unable to find a job and giving up the search or Baby Boomers retiring – neither of which reflects a booming labor market.

In fact, during the Obama era, the percentage of people in the labor force – either working or actively looking for a job – declined from 65.7 percent to 62.8 percent , while the unemployment rate declined from 7.8 percent to 4.7 percent.

That unemployment rate decline sounds good at first blush. But the telling point is that, had labor participation simply stayed at 65.7 percent, the unemployment rate when President Obama left office would have been 9 percent, or 1.2 percentage points *higher than when he assumed office.* People dropping out of the labor force, rather than economic prosperity, accounted for virtually all the decline in the unemployment rate during Obama's presidency.

Why were Obama's economists so wrong? Why didn't the economy experience the significant GDP bounce it should have following a deep recession? Why didn't unemployment remain below 8 percent following the stimulus?

The lesson here is that policy can matter more than economic cycles and that big government policies discourage business optimism and stifle economic growth. The simple truth is that business owners simply do not grow their businesses and create good-paying

---

If the government keeps its heavy hand on the economy, we may never fully recover.

---

jobs when they are concerned about what the government is going to do next to impede their success.

In fairness, the Democrat's primary goal was never economic growth or job creation. I'm sure they would have preferred it if the economy had grown as they forecast. It would have supported their belief that government-dominated economies can outperform the free market. But rather than economic growth, their primary goals were always government expansion and wealth redistribution – much as they are today. And they moved rapidly to advance those goals.

At the beginning of the Obama presidency, with the Democrats controlling both houses of congress and the presidency, they pursued these goals by statute. After 2010, when Republicans regained a majority in the House of Representatives, Obama continued to pursue those goals by working around Congress with "a pen and a phone" through executive orders and regulations.

A year after the "stimulus" bill, in March 2010, the Democrats passed the ironically named Affordable Care Act (ACA). They did so without a single Republican vote in the House or the Senate. The ACA placed control over much of the healthcare sector (about 17 percent of the economy) in the hands of government bureaucrats. Its mandates dramatically increased health insurance costs and deductibles, drove young people – who are essential to keeping health insurance costs down – out of the market, and encouraged businesses to move their work forces from full-time to part-time.

In July of 2010, Obama signed into law the "Dodd-Frank Wall Street Reform and Consumer Protection Act" (Dodd-Frank) saddling the financial sector with more regulations than it had seen since the Great Depression. Perhaps not surprisingly, it accomplished what it was intended to prevent. The "too big to fail" banks got bigger. Community banks (that typically fund small businesses) suffered. Many closed, unable to absorb Dodd-Frank's massive regulatory and compliance costs. The big banks, of course could afford those costs. It was actually a small price to pay for hobbling their community bank competitors.

In the November 2010 election, Republicans regained control of the House of Representatives and the progressive legislative onslaught thankfully came to an end. Unfortunately, the regulatory onslaught commenced.

During President Obama's eight years in office the Federal Registry of Regulations grew to an historic 100,000 pages. ACA regulations hampered the healthcare sector. Then–Labor Secretary (at this writing, DNC Chair) Tom Perez initiated an unprecedented flood of union-friendly and business-hobbling regulations. The National Labor Relations Board (NLRB) similarly promoted union agendas, the EPA adopted policies designed to increase energy prices, and the FCC even threatened to regulate the Internet.

It's helpful to think of regulations effectively as taxes: instead of government collecting revenue and spending it, businesses are forced to incur mandated costs directly. Except when legitimately protecting vital interests such as public safety, regulations primarily empower government bureaucrats and diminish economic growth.

With respect to actual prosperity-killing taxes, the ACA alone contained twenty tax increases as diverse as an individual mandate penalty for not having health insurance, a tax of 10 percent on tanning services, and a surtax of 3.8 percent on investment income for high earners.

In 2019, the nonpartisan Congressional Budget Office (CBO) issued a report that computed the annual average federal tax burden through 2016, President Obama's last year in office. The analysis included individual, corporate, payroll, and excise taxes. It found when Obama took office in 2009, the average federal tax rate was 17.3 percent. By 2016, the rate was 21 percent – a 3.7 percentage point increase that put the economy on the wrong side of the Laffer Curve.

As a result of this statutory and regulatory onslaught, and to the great surprise of the Obama administration's economists, rather than dynamically bouncing back following the recession, economic growth stagnated and the labor force declined. With employees competing for jobs – rather than employers competing for employees – wage growth was anemic.

It's worth noting that President Obama's economists were all sincere, professional, and well-educated people. They believed what they predicted, and they were genuinely surprised when their predictions did not pan out. The reason they were wrong wasn't because they lacked intelligence; it was because their premises were wrong, and their premises were wrong because they were blind both to the benefits of capitalism and to the danger which government poses to economic health.

It was workers who suffered. In fact, while yearly wages grew at 3 percent for the first three months of Obama's presidency, they never grew at 3 percent again for the remaining ninety-three months of his two terms in office. In February of 2015, Atlanta Fed researchers published a research paper appropriately titled "What's (Not) Up with Wage Growth?" A year later, the San Francisco Fed published an economic letter which again asked "What's Up with Wage Growth?"

Both would soon have an answer.

In November of 2016, Americans elected Donald J. Trump as president of the United States. To understand the positive impact of President Trump's policies on the economy and the labor market, it's important to also understand how both the business community and the liberal establishment reacted to his election.

The National Federation of Independent Businesses (NFIB) has been publishing a business optimism index for decades. According to the NFIB, it "blasted off the day after the 2016 election" – which tells us just about all we need to know about the impact of the Obama presidency on business growth. It

---

Bigger government isn't the path to economic renewal. It is the obstacle.

---

remained at or near historic highs through February of 2020 and the onset of the Coronavirus economic shutdown.

While the business community was rejoicing, liberals were predicting that President Trump's policies would bring about an economic catastrophe. Paul Krugman, noted Keynesian and anti-Trump economist at *The New York Times*, predicted on election night that the stock markets would "never" recover from Trump's win. CNN claimed that Trump's victory would "almost certainly tank" the stock market. The next day, *The Economist* stated that "the election could presage a longer slump" in the stock market.

As it turned out, on February 14, 2020 – just prior to the China virus crisis – the S&P 500 hit an historic high of 3,389.16, 63 percent higher than it closed on Election Day, 2016.

With respect to GDP growth, the CBO issued a report in January of 2017 forecasting 1.9 percent growth in 2018 and 1.6 percent in 2019. Under Trump, GDP growth clocked in at 2.9 percent in 2018 (beating the CBO's forecast by 53 percent) and 2.3 percent in 2019 (beating the CBO's forecast by 44 percent).

However, GDP was short of the Trump administration's 3 percent forecast, primarily due to the trade war with China, which disrupted supply chains and caused a slump in business investment. According to research by Federal Reserve economists, this disruption cost the economy about 1 percentage point in GDP growth. Obviously, with that percentage point, GDP would have exceeded the Trump administration's forecast.

Shortly before the China virus crisis, in December of 2019, the Trump administration finalized a Phase 1 trade deal with China. In January, Congress ratified the administration's trade deal with Mexico and Canada – The United States, Mexico, Canada Agreement – which replaced the much-criticized North American Free Trade Agreement. With these new and improved trade deals in place with our three largest trading partners, the anticipation was for increased economic growth. We will now have to wait for that positive impact until the Coronavirus crisis passes.

The labor market's response to Trump's economic policies was just as positive. Job creation proceeded at a fevered pace as Trump reversed virtually every economic policy Obama had implemented.

Following his inauguration and with the help of the Republicans in Congress, Trump immediately began eliminating the Obama era's prosperity-killing regulations. He promised to cut two existing regulations for every new one. In October of 2019, the White House announced that the Trump administration had actually cut 8.5 regulations for every new one, "slash[ing] regulatory costs by nearly $50 billion, with savings reaching $220 billion once major actions are fully implemented."

By the end of 2019, the page total in the Federal Registry of Regulations had dropped to just under 73,000, an over 25 percent reduction from Obama's nearly 100,000 pages.

The stimulative effect of this policy was far greater than simply the lower cost of the specific regulations that were repealed. It's

The novel Coronavirus created both a humanitarian and an economic crisis.

vital to understand that investors fear uncertainty and hostility from the government. The progressives in the Obama Administration increased regulations not just because they were trying to achieve social goals, but also because they actively distrusted private enterprise and wanted to micromanage it. They were effectively enemies of their own economy – or at least large sectors of it – and businesses never knew from where the next attack would come.

While President Obama increased taxes, President Trump and the Republicans cut them. On December 22, 2017, Trump signed the Tax Cuts and Jobs Act. It reduced tax rates for individuals and businesses, made America's corporate tax rate competitive with that of other nations, increased individual deductions and credits, increased the exemption for estate and gift taxes, and repealed the Affordable Care Act's individual mandate.

The labor market rapidly responded.

In March of 2018, the unemployment rate hit 4 percent for the first time in eighteen years. It would remain at or below 4 percent for the next twenty-four consecutive months, consistently hitting fifty-year lows of 3.5 percent to 3.7 percent from April of 2019 through February of 2020.

The strong labor market helped everyone. In 2019, unemployment hit lows not seen since the government began reporting the data for African Americans, Hispanics, Asians, and people with only a high school education. For women the unemployment rate hit a sixty-five-year low, and for teenagers (aged 16–19) it hit a fifty-year low.

Unlike the Obama years, this decrease in the unemployment rate was not caused by people dropping out of the labor force. To the contrary, while Baby Boomers were undoubtedly still retiring, labor participation *increased* under Trump from 62.7 percent in January of 2018 to 63.4 percent by February of 2020.

Perhaps most notably, also beginning in March of 2018 and continuing for the next twenty-four months, there were more job openings than people unemployed for the first time since the government began reporting the data. For seventeen of those months, there were over 1 million more job openings than people unemployed – a record that may never be equaled.

This was a very significant and dynamic change from the Obama era. When Obama left office, there were 1.9 million more people unemployed than job openings. A mere thirteen months later, job openings exceeded people unemployed for the first time and by 372,000. By July, job openings exceeded people unemployed by 1.1 million. In February of 2019 (the most recent month for which we have the data), there were still 1.1 million more job openings than people unemployed.

When employees compete with each other for a limited number of job openings, as they did under President Obama, wages stagnate or decline. When employers are competing for employees to fill job openings, as was the case under President Trump, wages increase.

As a result, in August of 2018 yearly wages increased 3 percent for the first time since April of 2009. They didn't stop there. Wages increased 3 percent or better for twenty consecutive months. The long-anticipated wage growth economists expected during the Obama years had finally arrived, nineteen months after Obama left office.

The bottom line is that a little more than a year after Trump took office, we went from an economy where the biggest problem was workers being unable to find good paying jobs to one where the biggest problem was businesses being unable to find enough workers.

Wages increased most significantly for blue-collar workers. A December 2018 report from The Conference Board found that it was harder to find blue-collar workers than white-collar workers, reversing a decades-long U.S. jobs market trend. Not surprisingly, the Bureau of Labor Statistics (BLS) consistently reported higher wage increases for production and non-supervisory employees than for supervisors.

The two lowest hourly wage sectors the BLS reports are "Retail" and "Leisure and Hospitality" (primarily restaurants and hotels). Wages for retail workers increased 4.9 percent in 2018 and 3.7 percent in 2019. For Leisure and Hospitality workers, wages increased 4.4 percent in 2018 and 4.2 percent in 2019. Although the mainstream media claimed otherwise, income inequality declined in 2018 (the most recent year for which we have the data) while median household income hit new highs.

Talk about a capitalist comeback!

Perhaps the most telling thing about the Trump Boom is the fact that, despite President Trump having reversed virtually every one of President Obama's economic policies, both Obama and his former Vice President

Joe Biden – now the Democrats' presumptive presidential nominee – have repeatedly attempted to take credit for it.

They deserve none.

President Obama pursued failed policies because of his mistaken belief that he could use government power to mandate prosperity through laws and executive orders. Unfor-

---

Milton Friedman recognized in the early 1960s that the deeper the recession, the stronger – and faster – the recovery should be.

---

tunately, that belief blinded him to the vast potential of enterprising individuals in a free market economy.

President Trump succeeded because he does not share that belief and did not succumb to the temptations of government power. Rather, Trump's policies relied on people striving to succeed unimpeded by the threat of an ever-expanding government.

Once the Coronavirus crisis subsides – and it will – if we want businesses growing, Americans returning to work, and wages soaring once again, President Trump's economic policies over the first three years of his administration are the roadmap for success.

When This Crisis Ends, Government Should Step Back ASAP

Most people seem to agree that a federal government–managed response is appropriate in a national crisis such as the current pandemic, particularly when the economic stress is the direct result of government action, such as its recent shut-down of the economy. But when this crisis ends, will we return to the freest economy in decades, the thriving private sector that, over the past three years, created jobs and rising wages across all income groups? Will we restore the labor market strength that carried with it a belief that the future held even greater promise than the past?

Or, will we move to a government-dominated economy that discourages individual initiative and dampens ingenuity? Where people succeed not by meeting the needs of others (consumers) but rather by meeting the demands of elites who distribute government largesse to those they deem worthy?

In other words, will we return to the economic stagnation that became the Obama era's "new normal" or the prosperity we came to expect under President Trump?

The Coronavirus Aid, Relief, and Economic Security Act (CARES Act), which Congress enacted to address the Coronavirus economic shutdown, contemplates a return to the vibrant and dynamic economy of the last three years once the crisis ends. The government programs it created to assist individuals and businesses have expiration dates or dollar caps. The checks to individuals are a one-time benefit. The increased unemployment benefits expire in four months. The

Small Business Administration's small business loans program has a $350 billion cap (which can be increased by further legislation). Various other provisions have similar end dates and monetary caps. It is crucial that any further programs Congress passes to address the crisis will similarly have expiration dates or monetary caps tied to the end of the crisis.

Of course it will be necessary for the government to manage to completion the emergency programs that are now underway. The Small Business Administration (SBA) is guaranteeing hundreds of billions of dollars in loans to small businesses to enable them to survive the pandemic. Those guarantees will have to be handled responsibly, like similar SBA lending programs. It will be both proper and necessary for the government, following its usual precedents, to recover as much for the taxpayer as possible, consistent with the commitments it has made and the purposes of the aid.

There is a danger that once the pandemic

abates, and government begins hungering for revenue, it will decide to extort every dollar it can and bring the hammer down on small businesses, which took the loans based on the government's promises but lack the resources to fight city hall. We promised loan forgiveness to the small businesses that kept the faith by keeping their workers on the payroll. It would be a mistake to double-cross them.

In a post-pandemic world, we will also need to address the implications of the massive increase to our federal debt caused not just by the pandemic response but by the decades of deficit spending that preceded it. Republicans and Democrats would do the country a tremendous service if, at long last, they entered into meaningful discussions about reducing federal spending and increasing government revenue without growth-hobbling taxes. In fact, even the prospect of a bipartisan consensus on reducing the deficit would have a beneficial effect on the economy as it recovers from the pandemic.

Otherwise, the prescription for economic

growth is clear. Three simple words hold the key to restoring prosperity as quickly as it tanked in the weeks following the economic shutdown, for creating millions of jobs, for reviving the careers that have been interrupted, for better wages for workers, for more money for education at all levels, for creating wealth that our charities and non-profits need, for stock market recovery so that our retirees are protected, and for surging the revenue of state and local governments:

Let capitalism work.

Let the free markets perform their magic. Let the dynamic energy of CEOs and line workers, professionals and technicians, entrepreneurs and accountants, restore the rising tide that was lifting all boats before the virus hit. I have no doubt that this will be the policy of the Trump Administration and Congressional Republicans. They created the boom of the last three years; they understand that while government has a vital role to play in helping the disadvantaged, it must allow the free market to work in generating the wealth that both the private and public sector need.

The question is this: What will the Democrats do? What about Joe Biden, Nancy Pelosi, and Chuck Schumer? Hopefully, they can resist the progressive zealots like Bernie Sanders, Alexandria Ocasio-Cortez (AOC), and Ilhan Omar: the people who, despite overwhelming and incontrovertible evidence to the contrary, still believe socialism works; the people who think Venezuela is a model; the people who seem completely oblivious to the economic experience of the last 100 years.

But, the signs aren't good.

When we emerge from this crisis, Progressives will doubtless argue that the government-directed virus-management model worked so well that it must surely work in other areas such as health care, education, housing, or environmental policy. In fact, even before this crisis began the Progressive's agenda included a massive and unfathomably expensive government takeover of the economy known as the Green New Deal. Bernie Sanders and Joe Biden

> *During President Obama's eight years in office the Federal Registry of Regulations grew to an historic 100,000 pages.*

both support it. Standing alone, the Green New Deal has the potential to expand the federal government beyond anything we have ever experienced, granting it power to control critical economic sectors such as energy, healthcare, construction, housing, and transportation.

This level of government expansion would require an expansive federal bureaucracy – well beyond even the Obama model – empowered through legislation and regulation and supported by unprecedented, growth-killing taxation. Bureaucrats would set economic goals discouraging both innovation and investment and rewarding only those who supported progressive policy goals. It would all but eliminate consumer choice, the free market force that drives competition and produces the prosperity and abundance that are the hallmarks of capitalism.

To be clear, this is not to say that all legislation or regulation intended to legitimately protect the environment – the water we drink and the air we breathe – is inherently wrong. Nor is there anything wrong with efforts to reduce the amount of carbon we pour into the atmosphere, through increased use of nuclear energy, natural gas, or renewables, when economically feasible.

But the manipulation of those goals to advance a collectivist agenda and replace our capitalist free market economy with a socialist economy, democratic or otherwise, is objectionable. To use the current crisis – a pandemic, nonetheless – as the vehicle to advance those goals is nothing short of despicable.

Yet, there can be no doubt that Progressives will cynically exploit the present fear to enact measures that would not pass in normal times. The tragedy for future genera-tions' prosperity is that, once such changes are in place, it will be virtually impossible to undo them. Through their comments and actions, we stand forewarned.

> After Democrats and Republicans had negotiated the CARES Act in the Senate, House Speaker Nancy Pelosi set up the Progressives' larger ideological argument by holding up the bipartisan bill's pas-sage. Her demands for passage included a lengthy progressive wish list of envi-ronmental, labor, political, and economic agenda items, essentially unrelated to the current crisis.

> Shortly after the CARES Act passed, thankfully *sans* her wish list, Pelosi appointed House Majority Whip James Clyburn as the head of a new select committee to oversee the Trump admin-istration's response to the pandemic – with subpoena power. As noted above,

Clyburn views the Coronavirus pandemic as "a tremendous opportunity to restructure things to fit our vision." Pelosi has put the progressive wolf in the government benefits hen house.

> In late March, AOC joined the effort to exploit the government's Coronavirus response. In a video for the Sanders presidential campaign, AOC advanced the theory that because the government is spending massive amounts to prevent an economic collapse during the pandemic, it can spend far more to fund progressive programs once the crisis comes to an end. According to AOC, "It's actually a fascinating progressive moment because what it's shown is that all of these issues have never been about how are you going to pay for it." In AOC's world, if we are willing to incur great cost to address the pandemic-caused shutdown, we should be unconcerned about the tremendous

costs of any other programs – such as the Green New Deal – once the pandemic ends.

> In an early April press conference, Democrat California Governor Gavin Newsom joined in the effort to set the stage for the post-pandemic progressive agenda. When asked about whether he saw the Coronavirus crisis as creating the "potential for a new progressive era," he responded "yes," stating that "we see this as an opportunity to reshape the way we do business and how we govern."

These comments demonstrate not only that Progressives intend to return to the big government growth and job-killing policies of the Obama administration, but that they will make every effort to put those policies on steroids both during and following the pandemic. Unlike President Obama, who ran as a left-leaning moderate, today's Progressives are making no effort to conceal their true intentions. If they succeed, our economy may well never recover, jobs may well never return, and, at best, wages will stagnate.

It is American workers who will suffer should we fail to take the Progressives' warnings seriously.

Conclusion

We can return quickly to the prosperity of the past three years if, and only if, we acknowledge the incredible potential of a people striving to improve their lives in a free market unhampered by excessive government interference. As I stated at the beginning, we need policies that encourage businesses to grow and hire rather than policies that encourage government dependence and discourage work. In sum, we need to return to President Trump's free market policies that led to the strongest labor market in modern history over the three years preceding the pandemic –

benefitting American workers to an extent rarely matched.

When the crisis ends, the choice will be ours.

© 2020 by Andrew F. Puzder

First American edition published in 2020 by Encounter Books,
an activity of Encounter for Culture and Education, Inc.,
a nonprofit, tax exempt corporation.
Encounter Books website address: www.encounterbooks.com

Manufactured in the United States and printed on
acid-free paper. The paper used in this publication meets
the minimum requirements of ANSI / NISO Z39.48–1992
(R 1997) (*Permanence of Paper*).

FIRST AMERICAN EDITION

LIBRARY OF CONGRESS CATALOGING-IN-PUBLICATION DATA
IS AVAILABLE